Mental Prison

I.D. Rose

Mental

Prison

Dedication

To my friends, family, and most importantly, my parents, Dr. Chantal and Jonathan Hacker, thank you for believing in me and supporting my work.

All my love.

Acknowledgements

I would like to thank my editor,
LuAnne Golden,
and the whole team at
Bethel 1808 Publishers,
who worked so hard to help me publish my
first book of poems.

Thank you so much for your patience and
guidance on this project.

Contents

Life is not a problem to be solved,
but an experience to be explored.

-Soren Kierkegaard

One-Sided Love

1. Another Output

Is there an extent to how much love a person
Can give?
Is there a point where a person can no longer
have room in his or her heart for anyone else?
Is there a region that becomes numb on the
Inside after too many people reside in one's
Heart?
Is it possible to feel nothing from feeling too
Much?
It is possible to have a void on the inside,
Desensitized from the sensitivity of the mind?
Each person makes it larger.

Whether I empathize or sympathize,
I have become desensitized.
I feel emotionally drained.

2. Can't

Can't write.
Can't think.
Can't feel.

Get out of my head.
Get out of my mind.
Get out of my thoughts.

Can't stop thinking about you.

• • •

3. *Together*

Your eyes stare at me with such clarity,
And yet I see nothing
Staring back at me.
Is it from this gentle depravity
From where I believed
There was nothing inside of me?
Is it me who is the cruel one?
Or, is it you, who is the cruel one
Who deceived my thinking?
Where is the connection
That is broken between our eyes
That stays broken
Because of this difference in our sight?
With I, seeing you,
And you, seeing me,
And my thoughts seeing something
Differently.
How can you not see, or
How can I not see
Anything
In the space between
Completely?
Does the word together....*exist?*

4. Family

As of late,
This feeling feels foreign.
There is no more love in the world.
The walls are silent.
The air is cold,
And the rooms are quiet.

5. Ever

If I could feel your touch,
Soft, gentle, pleasing feel
From cheek to heart,
Spread through my blood
As a part of me.

If I could say your name,
Clearly, truthfully, desperately,
Would you hear me?
Do these lips make an utterance
Only when you aren't around?

Hypocrite, wherefore art thou me?
With these bones,
I try day rise and day set,
But you still remain deaf.

My chest hurts around you.

My arms tremble, blood burning, mind
Cursing, limbs breaking, mind tearing,
Tearful silence, abusive babbling,
Sinful wrath, sinful passion, evil blood,
Against my sides.

End the pain I feel, or
I'll end it within this conclave
Of my feelings and me.

What would it feel like to be happy
Remaining for that moment?
Remaining for myself.
You have done this to me.
Can my heart even beat?
Does my flesh even bleed...
Numb with feeling,
Numb with love.

6. 365 Days of You

The sun on a cold autumn's day,
A cool breeze in a midsummer's nightmare.
A weed wrapped tightly around a wilting flower,
A fallen, frozen, branch dying in the snow,
Discarded parts again disregarded,
A moment of life, no more.
It's no longer the air that is cold.
When the seasons change,
The feeling doesn't go.
Whether everything is fading or already faded,
You still remain transparent.

I, still in remembrance of a memory,
Long forgotten by time,
The grass is gray with life.
As it seems, only the weeds flourish from my heart
When I speak,
And the flowers have been blown away by the
Spectating wind.
Even the seeds rained upon, have an indecisive
Moment after another.
Uncertainty crushes the neck of hope
And leaves the world barren with despair.
There's nothing left.
Slight apparitions of sight
Awake me from my slumber.
When will the rain stop?
When will you warm me, too?
Even though I have been shaken,
I can't bloom.

7. Feeling

Softly,
Burying the root of your sound
In the ground,
A tangled web of petals and
Thorns
Lost among the weeds.

8. Conflicted

You are exactly what I want
And exactly what I don't
need.

9. Think of Me

Do you think of me when you lie
Down?
Do you think of me when you're
Alone?

I think of the time we smiled
Together as if we shared a hidden
Secret.

I think of the time I stared off into
space while you stared off into me.
I remember loving you and
Not telling because I didn't want
Anything to change between us.
I remember putting this behind me,
Apparently.

10. Purple

Your voice,
Velvety soft against my ear,
Words of spoken truth whispered tenderly
Against my
Worries.
Gentle caress of wind and sky,
Oh, even lilacs could bloom in the
Air between us.

If only soil so rich could ever produce such a
Flower of such incomparable beauty in the sky,
The fragrance of our love permeates the very
Part of my soul,
And consumes me
Until I'm no longer breathing.
Until I turn my own shade of purple.
I could breathe you forever.

11. Lost Love

Sigh, sigh, and sigh again.
Did the once become the when?
Where are my feelings now?
So small, like wrens
Flying beneath my eyebrows.

12. Love

Thread-like strings
Both coarse and soft,
Plucked against my fingers.
Gentle.
Shaky noise becoming melodic
Slightly hypnotic; steady thrum
Of the instrument that I know.
An internal tone stepping lightly
Over wayward ears,
Sinking into the soul, slowly.
The repetition of every pattern
Layers over each and every verse
Until replaying the unsung chorus,
A dull, monotonous sound when
Replayed,
The final note holds,
And suddenly...
The heart breaks.

13. A Bittersweet

Wine and cheese?
Milk and cookies?
I prefer the sweeter of the two.
Aged by time.
Bitter with regret.
Even a sweet tooth is rotten to
The core.
And sometimes, something
Bitter
Can be regarded as sweet.

14. Youth

I was told to be
Careful.
I said
"Watch yourself before you fall
Head over heels."
And I decided to fall over the edge.
I don't feel like I'm falling.
Yet, gravity will pull me
Down,
And
I have yet to make an impact with the
Ground.
I can't remember a word
He said
I won't tell you if I'm okay
Truth or
Lie?
And I won't see *you*.
You don't know how I feel.
And, I don't know how I feel.
And,
I have yet to understand.

15. Locked

I can't tell the difference between
Love and fate.
My heart has been beating slower with
Every single passing wake.
My passion that makes my heart ache
Yearns for my life, ambrosia nectar to take.

My heart, sweeter than honeyed fruit,
Chokes my petals and breaks my roots.
Glazes my eyes with lies and truth,
Leaving my mind innocent,
The ignorance of youth.

Loving is a transgression of mine,
Whether I want it
Or neglect it over time.
But now, there is no more room.

16. Broken Heart

The words that pour forth
Out of my soul
Leave a bitter taste on my lips for you.
May it be for venom or antidote.

I feel thorns where my heart is.
If only you'd grace my sight again,
Then maybe my body wouldn't
Feel so hollow.

Your voice forever echoes off
These empty walls,
And reverberates painfully in my ears.

I'll visit you in my memories
Another day.

17. Muddled

I'm done with the false affection
Given the misdirection
That someone feels.
A way that I always yearned to feel,
Yet somewhere on the inside,
There is a place that doesn't respond
To attraction's gentle touch.
Even the tiniest bit will remind me
I am alive and breathing
And still wanting,

Yearning.

A smile is something you do while you cry.
A frown is something you do
When you laugh.
At least it feels right.

18. Matchstick

A single flame travels down the matchstick.
As it comes closer, I can feel the warmth burning my finger.
The matchstick becomes ashes.
My skin, blackened,
Enthralled by the flame,
I let it burn me.
As the mind becomes more agitated,
I feel less at peace.
A single flame burning brightly
The sensation becomes dull
As the small light flickers
In my hand, there remains the ashes of the match that lit the
flame.
And,
This friction....addiction of skin against grain,
I feel like I'm going insane.

Somewhere,
Some
Thing,
Is saying my
Name.

Yellow,
Orange.
Red
And Blue.

With this feeling,
What am I supposed to do?

19. 4:42

To write about heartbreak
When a heart hasn't been broken,
It's breaking from love,
A love so strong even the heart gives way.

The feeling becomes numb on the inside.
There would be butterflies,
But they choked on the bittersweet nectar
Of a wilting flower,
Suffocated breathless,
And starved on absent affection.
A one-sided love, the simple butterfly
A feeble heart, the fragile wings.
The wanting, the thirst to drink of the
Sweet, sweet poison,
Sweet, because it is bittersweet, and
Nevertheless, is a poison.

The flower, the you I can't attain,
Flourished with color and spirit in the light
Of youth.
This heart breaks because of it.
One day, a promise was made,
And words refuse to break their meaning,

For this stupid heart remembers
What was said.

Still...
Why wouldn't the flower spread its petals
Soft, open smile when I have these feelings,
Brewing inside of me like a toxic mixture of
Acid and fire?

The pain of being in love.
And thus is the complex logic of my moral,
Which corrodes at this feeling
Like a mother with a child.
As the result of parenting, the feeling
Becomes repressed,
And then this heart braces to be torn apart,
But instead, it alights cautiously on the
Flower
And doesn't proceed to drink.
The poetry of a feeling desired
Remains unread.

This beating blood is stained fatally red.

20. Icy Heart

Frost covers the grass in a thin layer of
Crystal glass.
A drop of the seasons.
Rain
Snow
Dew
Mist.
Can I be honest with my heart
Before I melt away
Into nothing?

If it rains in winter, it snows.
Watching the snowflakes
Disintegrate against the palm of my
Hand,
Before I can see the crystals form.
A warm winter night storms.
And this layer of me melts.

21. Anticipation

These days pass pretty fast.
These ones in particular.
My feelings and thoughts
Are both...perpendicular.

It's singular.
Denoting the word
For us..."together," a continuum.

Life is a song in my heart
Beating...in time...with the clock's pendulum
I oscillate between love and fate.

Reverse

The beat of time
Makes the days go backwards.
I've been pleading, hoping
But nothing is getting faster.

22. Him

I like the way he looks now

Uncomposed, ruffled, unkempt,

Unfiltered, uncontrolled, and free.

His hair is a mess.

I've saved his expression in my memory.

I've never seen this side of him before.

I wouldn't want to forget this face.

In these moments

When I catch him off guard,

I see someone else

Who has been caged inside.

The way his face breaks into a wide grin

The way his eyes overflow when he's happy

The intelligent look he mimics when he jokes around

The look he takes inside when no one is watching

The way he shuts off the rest of the world

● ● ●

The way he speaks through his eyes.

The feeling I get inside my chest

Euphoria

At any new discovery,

Realization,

Interpretation,

Of him.

The fear I feel

When I've overstepped my bounds

Trying to urge that person outside

Of the conformity of himself.

I overthink his composition

Overtaken by the thought of him

When he spends time with me.

The simple, yet undiscovered,

Him.

23. The Fabricated

I think I've had more conversations with
You inside my head.
It feels easier to open my heart
To myself.
It's beating,
It's aching,
And I don't know how I feel.
What is this?
I feel like a child inside someone else's
Body.
What are these emotions I feel?
They conflict me over and over again,
And I feel safer inside my head
Than I am with you.
Somehow, your presence is hypnotic,
And you take me somewhere where I
Don't think I want to be.
This pointless affection,
Solely directed,
At the one who isn't even you.

● ● ●

24. One-Sided

I felt it slip
Ever so tenderly
Fallen
And then
It was gone.
I want it back.
Come back.
It hurts without you.
Inside me,
You became my heart.
How could you leave?
Come back.
Can I call you from the depths
With the sweetest whisper?
Or will I remain here,
Empty?

Bit by bit, you tear to me pieces.
The dream I once had
Is torn by your voice.

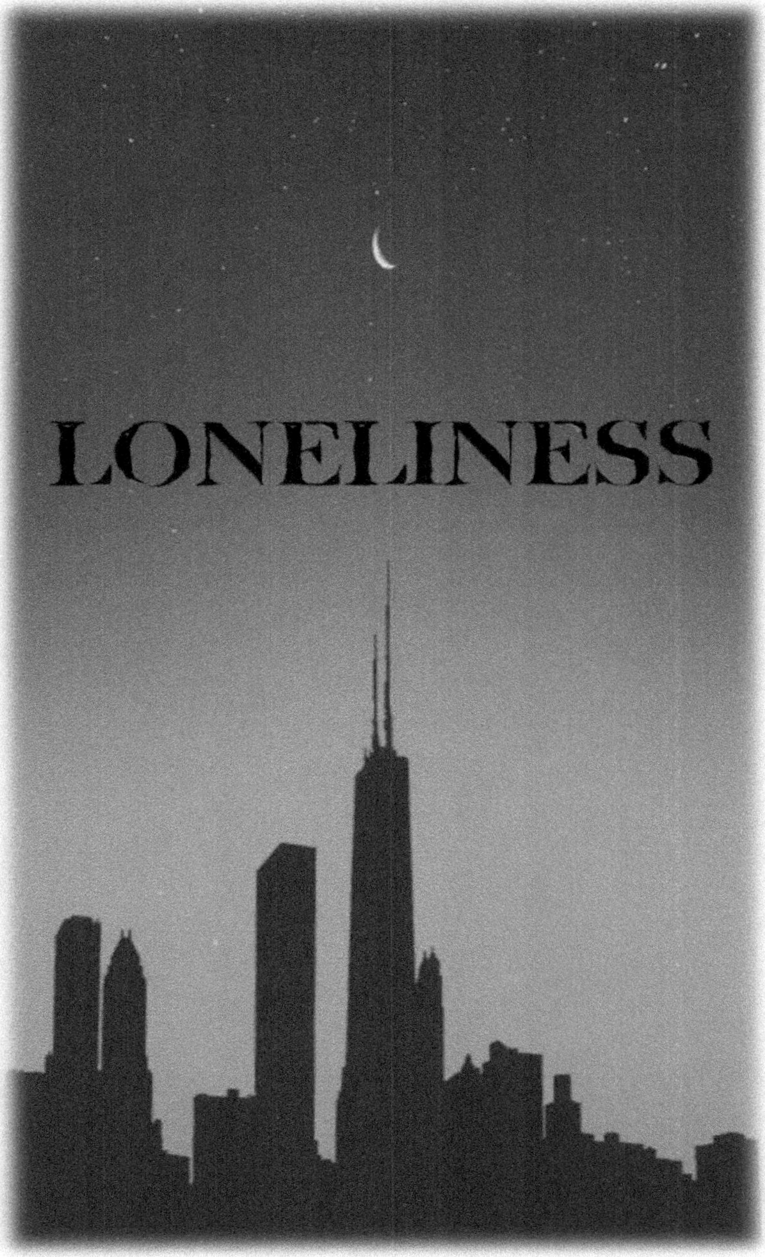
LONELINESS

1. When I Am Alone

Come hither solitude.
Let's talk about the things that we usually do,
And let's sit around and laugh
At all the pain and sorrow
When my eyes are blackened blue.

So, come hither solitude.
Let's sing about the dumb things I usually do,
And let's sit and contemplate the mess that is me
Until I am through with seeing you.

So, come hither solitude.
Come, so that I can care for you.
In the silence that is true,
I will always be with you.
To be with you,
Just me and you,
With me in you.

So, come hither solitude.
And let's laugh about the things that we usually do,
Until my eyes are low,
And my chest is hollow,
From having you,
With me in you.

So, come hither solitude.
When I'm alone,
Let's sit around.

2. Quarantine

It's like no day is ever Monday.

Some part of life has been put on pause and some part of living feels off.
Every day is either Friday or Saturday or someday by its means, and
Monday, no matter how terrible it seemed, was always the start of the
new week.

It's like no day is ever Monday; No day feels dreaded the same way.
Yet, we're found drifting in and out of peaceful terrors and fitful dreams
within the same few days on repeat.
All our contemporary joys and aspirations are temporarily maintained and
yet, the constant drag of monotony lags behind these never-ending days.
And wayward skies seem so blue.
The night sky is clear and bright is the moon
With its blinding, vibrant and hopeful light, the fragmented day turns into
night.

Yet, a day like Monday doesn't feel the same.
Does Monday even feel the change?
How habits, new and old, have flourished and welcome and unwelcome
thoughts have returned?
Or how the daily routine has been furnished, and the old one has been
deferred?

No, day is ever Monday.
The morning is a start of its own.
Monday is now just a memory that resides in this time alone.
The same day that tagged along so closely to Sunday and made the
week feel long gone.

It's like no day is ever Monday.

Will Monday come again?

3. Worry

The imminent presence over my
shoulder,
Always watching, calculating,
Disembodied, colorless smile,
Visible apparition of my emotions,
Sealed tightly, securely inside.
My heartbeat speeds up,
Faster and faster within my
Chest as I fall asleep,
Awake, watching, checking,
Sudden pain and release,
My chest...within or without,
Blinking,
Seething,
Quiet,
Yet it isn't silent,
Present, looming over my bed,
Day...and...night.

● ● ●

4. Shadow

At night,
After the sun goes down,
I can see the after image of my arm.
The colors are hazy.
My eyes hurt.
There's no reason to go to sleep.
When I stretch my hand out,
I reach as far as I can go.
There's an after image of
My hand, too.
When I walk to go somewhere,
There's an after image of me as well.
However, my after image is always
With me.

5. Letters

Before I speak,

I need to collect my thoughts,
Quietly written down on a piece of paper,
Softly spoken to my-self,
Sealed inside a memory:
Message sent.
Asking,
Do you remember me?
Are these pieces of paper all I have left?

Retentive about the letters left on my desk.

6. Silence

Synonymous with
   Quiet,
      Still,
         Moments of
            Tranquility.
Something expressed
   As a single
   Word
   Yet,
   Expressed
  Without a sound.

Quietly,
     Tenderly,
       Without
         Meaning
            Or
              Warning.
          Silence
       Steals
     Into
   My
Mind,

Bringing forth the feelings often reserved
For these moments of quietude
As they come together,
They pile on top of
one another,
Draining
Away
Into
A
Specific place
Somewhere
Inside.

And somewhere,

I can feel it.

Silence.

What is this?

It beckons me...closer

To a place
Where forgotten things fester
Hungrily for a piece of my thought,

• • •

Stolen from the reserves of my mind.
Yet, comes forth my medicine
Of having nothing to say
A temporary joy
Of existing in another time.
When I recall these moments of

Silence.

Somehow, it fills the space on both sides
Well enough to pacify any tear, laugh
Smile or frown.

It paralyzes these emotions.

A moment of silence,

The absence of sound,

And the absence of

Mind.

The silence lapses into a faint
Ringing that becomes louder by the

• • •

Second.

A white sound pulsating in my ears.

I feel the pitter-pat of feet repeating over and over only to realize it is my own blood rushing past my ears.

Again, the footsteps come closer.

The footsteps become

Heavier.

Louder.

The sound becomes

This

feeling

Keeps

Pumping

With

My

Blood.

Different colors

Come over   my face
Like a TV,   static crackles
The image,   out of focus
Flashing colors,   a blank
                    Screen

Pulsating through everything

Everything

Everything

I can't hear.

Then again, silence doesn't have a sound.

7. One Decade and Three Years

At the moment,
I am breathing,
And it hurts to breathe.
I want to speak to the person at my side,
But I don't want to talk.

I think upon who I can talk to,
And I find no one.

Not an ear paid for,

And not the ear wished for.

So, I looked up to God,
And hoped he would answer
With no reply,
I cried out again.
He is there,
But I don't hear his voice.

The noises on the outside and
Inside of my head are too loud
For me to be able to listen.

So, I held my breath for a second,
And I felt relief,
A tight embrace around my neck.

Then, I realized that the feeling in my heart was
The desire for death.
I opened my mouth to breathe again

• • •

Because I had to.
But for just that one second,
I felt as if everything could stop.

There was silence in my mind,
And peace within my heart.
For once, after all these years,
I am only one decade and three years old.

People shake their heads at me.

What do I know?

The thought of the deed and the seconds before.

I know my life, and the length I've lived.

I've cried.
I can't think about it without feeling my body's
Response.
The agony inside my mind to the sorrow in my cells.

It's my secret.

I can smile
I can laugh
Even someone like me can make others do the same.

I feel nothing.

I feel empty inside,
And I don't know why.
Everything is so numb.

The space is empty
And my mind is too full.

Everyone tells me that the remedy for insensitivity is to
Cheer up
And to be optimistic.
A simple home remedy for anyone who has a happy
Home.
Take it daily until the symptoms begin to show.
Bright eyes
And high hopes.

I've been trying to be so.
As the earth tilts on its axis,
The wheel of misfortune turns.
One decade and three years,
My life could be but a chance second more.
My heart is filled
With every tumult of my existence

Only a small portion to make me laugh
And the majority to make me cry

The only real thing is pain.
It makes *me* feel real.

At my age,
What am I to know?
For a person who has only lived
One decade and three years short of a lifetime.

DEPRESSION

1. Time Keeps Passing.

A second to a minute,
The minutes to an hour,
Twenty-four hours in a day.

Times keeps passing.

It's always the same,
But never the same.

A moment of bliss
Followed by a sorrowful kiss goodbye.

Then, time passes again.

The time spent is the time best taken
Memories are the recordings of the past
That get more scratched up with age
Until dull spots form in places where you
Once believed you would never forget,

But time passes,
And it will pass you on.

2. *Breakdown*

I can't do this anymore.
I just want to leave and never return.
I don't miss this feeling.
It's coming back again.
All I can hear is my name
Over and over and over again!
The sound is deafening,
But the air is silent.
Relieve me of this pain,

Please!

I'll be patient.
I'll wait.
I wish I could be somewhere far away.

Far away...
Far away...

I just want silence.

It would feel so nice to have my mind
Be silent.

3. Breathe

And my heart cries

These crimson tears

Of a solemn shade of red

Stained against the hollow.

Frustrated...

Desperate...

Caving in.

4. It's...There

On the verge of tears, release.
Open the faucet and let the water slide over
My face, my neck and
Across my shoulders and down my arms,
And watch it pool in my hands
Like a puddle of thoughts.

Drowning is my soul.
The feelings I have left
Drown in these memories.

I release the water, but my hands fill up
Again.
It keeps on coming back to me.
My voice becomes hoarse, nothing more than
A whisper
Among my thoughts, there is nothing left for
Them to be.
Whether they manifest or remain a remnant
Of the past,
They linger like the clouds, hesitant to leave
The sky during a storm.

• • •

How to be mute and still have the ability to
Speak.
My body trembles.
I can't move.
I can't think.
I imagine someone who could hold me,
And I hold myself.

Passing day, a familiar ache,
These memories have a sound.
Like a marionette led by a puppet master,
They speak to me in their mocking, laughing,
Lilting, and littling way.

I push the thoughts...down.

The farther away they are, the less I can
Hear.

The feeling breaks, and I don't have to
Remember.

• • •

5. Can't Sleep

When the lights are off,
I find myself doing things differently,
Differently
In the dark.
Every corner becomes a spider's web.
Every shadow becomes a lingering person.
Every sound becomes the maniacal taunting of the
Creatures who wish to hurt me.
It's only my imagination,
Maybe,
That the creatures want to find their way inside of
Me.
They've made themselves well-acquainted with my
Brain's algorithm,
And like a virus, they want to change every, single
Thing,

Error...
Error...
Error!

6. Not Needed

Maybe I shouldn't exist right now,
The scene plays better without me,
Watching the images before my eyes,
I think of anywhere else I could be.

7. Loss

There was a certain
Day,
And then there was
You
And the sudden day after
And then the next day came
And the day after that came about
And the days after that came
Around,
But,

You never came again.

8. Parallel Worlds

Sometimes I want to keep sleeping
Then maybe, I think to myself,
I'll wake up in a different reality.
In a different part of my timeline
Acted by another me
In another place at another time
With a different outcome
Another reality,
Another possibility beside another possibility.
Wouldn't that be nice?

9. Eternal

Listening to the same song
Over and over
Until my mind ceases to think
Until the words are unable to form,
And until everything is drowned
In endless sound.
My ears pound against my skull,
And the feeling numbs into nothing.
Unable to cry out and
Unable to listen
I remain,
Listening to the same song.

• • •

10. Or

As the leaves fall,
A gust of wind picks them up
And carries them away
Until they fall
Inevitably
To the
Ground.
Meanwhile, a flower grows,
Weeds choke,
And people don't watch where they step.
The sky starves it,
And surprisingly,
The flower wilts
And is crushed.
Whereas the butterfly
That began as a caterpillar,
Begins to fly
Up and up into the air
To a place far away
Where it knows to die.

11. Jade

I wasn't there when she died,

Hands on her fur

Waiting for this all to be a lie.

I scream and scream,

But no one heard me.

No one knew.

I keep waiting for the box to come alive,

But there's no breath inside.

My hands can't move.

My thoughts can't write.

Sitting outside your cage and wondering where I

Left you,

When I left you between the clay.

I wish I could have buried you deeper than my

Hands would let me dig.

12. Bedtime

My alarm goes off.

Breathe in, breathe out.

After all these dreamless nights,

My eyelids will close again to darkness.

If only I could stay asleep and not have to

Keep waking up,

But I can't.

I have places to go.

When I don't,

I'll ignore the hurting in my sides

And keep sleeping.

13. Limbo

The descent into madness
  Is slow and grieving
    Like the whisper of heaven
      Among the souls of the deceased.

    Never risen
      But never fallen
        Suspended in between
          Arms outstretched to embrace the air
            Reaching towards the clouds in the sky,
              Tears covering their eyes
              As a tear follows another
              Down their faces

In a feeling,
    It was like their life became a looking glass,
      And the life reflected back was backwards.

    Their lives were like a film that plays for
        No one and nothing, on and on without an end.

The weight in their hearts bloomed
Like a flower made of stone.
It threatened to sink them
Into the void.

Their cries of despair echo
  Off empty walls
    And disappear into the nothingness,
    The something that remains.

What is it like to not exist
  When nothing exists,
    And the nothing that surrounds
      Is never-changing?

    In a space where reality is stilled
    And all reason is quiet,

      In a place where all things are unfulfilled
      And all beings are silenced,

They are the ones who could not
Make it into the next life.

When there was something left of *them*,
  These lamentations of their heart,
    Pressing against the pit in their soul

The descent of a broken mind
  Devoid of any thing left to pertain to *them*
    A vessel with no owner
      Somewhere within the remains of *them*.

Never descending,
  But never ascending,
    Suspended in the shadows.

In the end,

    Was the person inside them *dying*

      Or was that feeling already of death?

14. Desensitized

Make it feel real.
Make it,
Feel, real.
Make me feel before I die a lie.
Make me feel.

I want to write my fantasy.
Alone with
Just you and me.
Together,
Inside my
Reality.
Please,
Even if it hurts,
Even if I cry,
I just want to feel alive.

Please let me breathe!
Please let me sigh!

Evoke a feeling deep inside
Whether it's painful or not.

15. A Look Upon the Shoulder

A look upon the shoulder
My eyes narrow
As a tear finds a way down my neck.

This darkness contains my self
As this emotion I identify as sadness
Trickles away
Into these tears that surround me.

They form a sea of regret
That threatens to hold me
To tell me there is nowhere to go
Though, when was there ever?

An exit accepts the thought of escape.
An entrance is where it all begins.
My eyes strain until they can strain no more.
However, there is no such thing that exists
Anymore.

Crying without a sound
To remind me that I am,
Crying.

Smiling in vain.
What is running down my face?

16. Voices

I don't feel quite like myself.

To explain the constant whispering
Perhaps lingering
Of the voices inside my head.
I find it hard to think clearly
Through the headache that never ends.
The voices refuse to cease.

The murmuring begins in the morning.
The voices will talk to me
They will condemn.
They will demand.
They will mock.
They will leer.
They will talk badly about the people I know.
And they will threaten me with my worst fears.

They tell me they know me better than anyone else,
And they tell me they are the only ones who care,
And they tell me I'm nothing, and that I don't deserve
To be here.

And until the din of their voices becomes dim,
I can't hear anything.
I don't know how to feel about their company.
I want for my mind to be quiet,
But I'm scared of silence
And forgetting that this is a part of me.

• • •

An old fantasy comes to mind now and then.
An encounter with a beast that would have enough
Pity to take the life out of me
Would leave me ripped apart.
The teeth that would cut my skin like paper,
Grind my bones to dust,
And scrape the marrow of my bones clean
Would be enough.

And blood, like the smoke of incense, would taint the air
Like a perfume to me.
It is more out of love for my-self than out of hate
That I would want to cease this mindless headache.

The voices already surround me.
They suffocate me, steal me, break me,
Bruise me, take me
And eat me alive day by day.
What I feel and what I've felt take me in.
And the voices,
Those nameless, faceless demons that play with me,
Stay.

I wonder if other people can hear them.
Screaming.
I worry if other people can see them.
Pleading!
No one can tell, so
No one would know,
And no one needs to, though.
It's fine.
Truly, I'm fine,
And everything is alright.

• • •

17. Alone With My Phone

Everything is okay inside the walls of my
Phone.
Hands against the smooth and even screen,
I don't need anything else,
And I'm not alone with myself.
At least there's something else here with me.

18. Some Thoughts

Is it possible to know what death is
Before you have even died?
This off-beat, aching feeling in my chest
This pounding sensation in my breast
Of the sorrowful anticipation,
Then the quiet acceptance of life,
Wondering if I will lay at peace
In peace forever
One day.

19. At Least

I can still cry.

It's one thing I retained.

It makes me glad...when I see my tears.

It's nice to know I can

Have something left.

And the feeling I get

When I don't make a sound,

Makes this loud silence become quiet.

What a sweet pain.

Isn't it such a sorrowful delight?

20. End

As I walk along this worn path,
I feel that I am alone.
I look back at my shadow,
A shadow I call my own.

Even though I have eyes,
I feel that I can't see.
The world before my eyes is gone,
And the only one who knows is me.

As the darkness begins to near,
I feel the very rhythm of my soul,
Shedding my tears of longing,
At all my feelings untold.

A secret embedded in my heart
That will be the end of me
Whispered into the flowing wind,
My last-and-only-plea.

Will I be remembered?
A question in itself
That no one will be able to answer
No one except, myself.

In this spoken vanity, I will cry,
Wishing someone would answer me.
However, I have always been alone,
Alone for my eternity.

This worn path that I have walked alone
Now disappears behind me.
In this world that I have lived in,
There is no one beside me.

For truly, I haven't shed more tears,
For this is my sorrowful end.
My last words have been spoken,
So this is my...

The End!

21. Holding It All Back

I want to cry.

If I were a raincloud,
I could let it rain,
Let the tiny beads of precipitation fall down
My face.

At the moment, it's just a raincloud,
Dominating the space of my sky
That makes me think this way.

The cloud remains,
Sincerely waiting to see my resolve dissolve
Through the cracks of my will.

I won't cry over a tiny rain cloud.

It's just a little rain cloud.
It's just a little downpour.

At least for a moment,
I want to cry.

THE IN-BETWEEN

1. Belief

All I wanted to be was happy.
For a long time I believed
That happiness,
Once achieved,
Would satisfy the need
I felt inside.
But happiness
Didn't seem to be for me.
Even if things went perfectly,
What I imagined
That would make me complete
Left me hollow
And solemn to keep.
Somewhere in between,
I was caught,
Bound by the thing
I desperately sought.
Nothing could satisfy
The void beneath
Unless the light
Came to reap.
And the void inside,
Felt so deep.
And to be complete,
I didn't need what I thought I needed.
All I wanted to be was happy,
But happiness...
Wouldn't...
Complete me.

2. It Is What It Is

When did I have to become dissatisfied
With myself
To change who I am?
What was ever wrong with being
Just me?

> It's hard to find the reasoning.
> There's no meaning
> In being someone I am not.

And yet,
There may have been a time when it felt
Necessary.
I have decided
That being myself is what I'll do.
Title it as you wish,
And to me, it'll be nothing more
Than a useless label.

• • •

3. In Conclusion

Knowing what it's like to drown
To have my very last breath
Drawn out from between my lips
In the depths of a foreign river,
And dream about that trauma
For months on end,
Doesn't make me hate water,
Even though I remember.

4. Ambivalent Bloodlust

Lately,
I've been having episodes.
While walking quietly, head down towards the
floor,
My eyes waver as a single thought beckons me
Unsuspectingly, closer, enticing me deeper into
the hidden depths of my mind to reveal violent
fantasies.

The reversal of each and every one of my
memories
In which I was the tormented now as the
tormentor.

Unhinged, raw, unfiltered desire wets my lips,
savory sweet.

It lingers, coursing through my veins like energy.
My vision becomes a tunnel, and all I can see is red.

My teeth chatter, and my arms become tingly,
A single, mindless, maddening command
Chants over and over to *LET GO*.
That senseless intent breaks loose of my body,
Leaving me limp and aware of my pause.

Weak and scared of myself, I try to forget,
Yet the aftertaste left in my mouth is bitter,
Rotten, and metallic.
It takes me to bed, but I can't sleep on this bed of indecision
As this monster rears its Ugly head.

5. *This is Not a Poem*

I saw a painting
Of a photo deftly drawn.
Antique in appearance
And young in its composition.
Simplistically beautiful.

6. *Reveal*

Until a dream bleeds another color,
It's hard to see what you earnestly desired
Before your eyes
In the moment of truth.

7. *Layers*

Sometimes
I hold my hand to my heart
And,
I can't feel
My heartbeat.

8. I Can't Be Me

I'll be honest with myself
And be honest with you
About being dishonest with
Myself.

9. People

Those around me will reveal their
Sinful lies.
The ones they whispered in my
Ears as I slept.
These voices that haunted my
Dreams into nightmares,
The creatures who smiled as I
wept.

10. For You

I don't know what to do.
I don't know what to say.
This came without a manual
Or any directions to lead me
On my way.

What do you want to hear?
What would make you smile enough?
I think I am all out of jokes.
My heart can't seem to rise up.
What would be right?
What would be the best thing to say?
I'm panicking; I can't find anything,
For you on this darkened day.

I don't have any answers,
But I refuse to go.
Even if I don't have the answers,
At the very least, I'll stay.

11. Lullaby

If you would tell me a bedtime story
Put me to rest with your soothing oratory
Silence my thoughts with your words,
I would finally
Go to sleep.
The shadows would disappear.
I would feel safer at your side,
In the night atmosphere.
If you would whisper gently in my ear,
Cast aside all my worst fears
And lay a gentle tale in my heart,
I would finally,
Go to sleep.

12. My Life

This
American drama
Is so
Badly
Edited.

13. Left Behind

Why am I not talented at anything I do?
Whether it be at work
Or whether it be at school?

Why does my hard work
Not show?
Why does my smile shrink,
And my frown grow?

What is this feeling?
It feels like is eating my soul,
Gnawing at my insides,
Telling me *no more.*

What is this feeling
That makes me want to hide?
What is this feeling
That's eating me inside?

14. Full

The faults found in someone
Isn't always her fault.
But how much someone can take
Has a limit,
And I'm full.

15. Blossom and Thorn

Flowers begin as seeds that germinate, grow
And pollinate.
Any of the beauty we see starts from just a
Little, tiny seed.
Every seed is different,
And from each blooms a different flower.
Even if that much is true,
What truly causes a seed to
Rise from the Earth?
Before it reaches the surface,
Won't it expand all its energy,
And fall short of what it could be?
To get through all the dirt,
What does the flower receive?
After the wind threatens to break it's stem,
The sun overwhelms it with too much heat;
The weeds grow around its base,
And the rain drowns it again and again.
What does the flower believe?
Did it ever know that it could bloom?

16. Moonlight Thoughts

Light and dark,

An entire life in darkness
Makes one wonder about light.

If there is darkness,
There must be light.
Darkness is everywhere.
And so is light.

Darkness isn't the same as light.
It doesn't exist without,
And the other cannot exist...with.
That is to say if each existed at all.

It's like the bond shared through
Blood and war
The good against the bad.
Blood doesn't shine,
And the memory of war doesn't fade.

Without either,
There is nothing in the world.
Nothing of the dark

And nothing of the light
Leaves nothing.

When left having nothing but
Nothing at all,
Our world would become the very
Nothingness that resides inside us.
Without the visible bond that makes our
World go round.

Together,
In silence
We would fade away.
Because nothingness
Is what fills the void.
A world without anything
Is a lost world.
And a lost world,
Is another "nowhere."

Therefore, if one spends an entire life
Dwelling in the land of light,
One will wonder if darkness,
Exists.

If there is more light than darkness,
Will darkness disappear?

Is there true darkness without light?

Darkness moves quickly.
One is in the shadows of the planet of
Oneself, and one another
Across the hidden surfaces of the world.
In the eyes of a stranger, a close friend
And the depths of one's pupils.

And yet, even the shadows
Outcasted in the outskirts,
Remember the feel and touch of
Daylight.

Sol
And
Luna
Stranded across the sky,
One after the other appears to hide.

Even on a particular starry night,
The light is not so dim.
Nor is the air so thick,

That one cannot feel
Within.

Under the watchful eyes of the ticking
Clock...

Life is not an endless timeline.
It is the time before the end
When everything
Will truly be gone
And nothing will remain
One day.

Light appears to be infinite.
Like color or sound,
It is limited by what can't be seen or felt.
It's visible and invisible.
Physical but improbable,
And darkness disappears in its presence.

17. Over

We talk to keep the conversation
Going,
But neither of us have the right words
Anymore.
Are we even speaking to each other
Anymore?

What's this airless noise
That goes around my head?
Wouldn't it be better
If we talked honestly instead?

I put on a smile
Like I'm listening.
I can't bear to hear your voice
Anymore.
Everything is muddled.
I don't understand anything
That's going on between us.

18. Makeshift

How many more stitches till it all
Becomes plastic?
I didn't choose the pieces that everyone
Else picked.
I'm still a person, and with these pieces
I'll become whole...right?
Finally, a doll that everyone around
Likes.
Why does this feeling weigh heavy on
My chest?
Pin pricks and needles through my
Breast.

19. Wordless

There's always a feeling
That we need to describe
Whether it be about the color blue,
Or about the look in someone's eye.

Sometimes that feeling is nameless,
And then sometimes it has a name.
But, when that feeling is gone,
Everything feels the same
Unless you can't feel at all.
You'll always know a feeling you can't
Explain
Even if it's such a simple notion,
These nameless feelings can drive you
Insane.

When did life become about feelings
When everything could be without feeling,
And everyone could be unfeeling
About the feelings they felt toward
The little things they weren't seeing, or are
Seeing?

Now, then, and later,
It all feels the same.
But what is that feeling that we can't give a
name?

Maybe we just want to find some
Individuality
In our very own personalities?
Maybe that's why everyone strives to be
Noticed?

And no matter how fake, or how unreal
They become,
They continue existing as the individual
They

Aren't.

And why?

Why?

20. Seconds at a Time

They say it can take a second,
For someone to break.
One second,
A second too late.

Life is a dream.
Death is a fate.
The difference could take a second,
Wait.

Keeping your hopes high
Even with all these dreams you make
One realization:
The time it takes.

Think to know and
Remember to realize
That it is only the passing time,
And that every moment materializes.

21. Paradox

Lovesick, but loveless.
What is the emotion I yearn for,
But the emotion I detest?

Colorful, yet colorless
Thinking of something, and I regress to a
Time when color was monotone.

Thoughtful, but thoughtless,
The one semblance,
I confess.

To be....

Careful, but careless
A situational contradiction.

Helpful, but helpless
To others, then to myself I am...

Meaningful, but meaningless.
A moment is like a shadow,
Nevertheless.

22. *Confessional*

An embrace is unwanted.
To close the distance between suddenly,
Can feel like an invasion.
It leaves my mind to wander and worry
That someone will try to hold me,
And end up wrapping their arms around my
Heart and leave their mark there.

Proceed with caution.
I just don't want anything
To be in a place I don't want it to be.
Otherwise, I give in.

The fear co-exists alongside the aching need
For comfort of which the absence weighs
Down my thoughts.
I'm not used to it.
Even if I am scared of going beyond myself,
And ever still afraid to bring someone closer,
I could say that I don't mind.
Touch me.

23. Blindsided

There,
The mislead children
Followed the crooked path
Martyred by the thieves of their heart.
Carefully, they take my eyes out of my
Head
And replace the sockets with the
Afterimage of a picture
That says about a couple of words.
Riddles, couplets,
A poetry of misunderstood meanings
Thousands of interpretations based on
Interpretations
To which I cannot interpret.
Whether or not I can paint the picture,
It still remains in pieces.

24. *Confessional 2*

Guests visit my house to inspect
Every floor, every surface, and every room.

In the last room, waiting,
I expect a discussion to form around me.
Achievements, failures, tendencies,
Behaviors,
Each word seems to coil around me and inject
Itself into my head.

These guests come uninvited,
Excited,
Delighted to stay over a little too long.

I turn blind eyes away and think about the
Confinement of my seat at this table.

Sweat gathers beneath my collar,
My sleeves, and my stomach
As I talk carefully about
My day and try to correctly articulate
My hours away.

I would be lying if I say
I don't want to leave,
But I can't.

Each voice with a conversation point
That I become weary to adhere to.

I feel empty.

I desire to see someone, *proud of me*,
Not as a trophy.

Yet, I have become one

Who is struggling to breathe

And forgetting...
To get out of...
My head.

25. Overwhelmed

Unknowingly,

It may have been temporarily
-Temporary,

There, only
-Momentarily,

There, only barely,
-Apparently,

Reflection in transparency,
Leads to the invariability,
Of reality's fantasy,

To one's inability

To deal with the entirety.

26. I Didn't Know

I was alive,
But he was dead.

They told me he was dead,
And he died without me.

I was desperately trying to see within,
And he made sure I couldn't see without.

Everything that happened around him,
Still remains a mystery to me.

Yet, he told me *It's okay* that one last
Time,
And I made the mistake of believing his
Smile,

But he was smiling for me,
Not for himself.

● ● ●

27. Thinking

My mind
Silent, but thinking.

My words
Pointless, with meaning.

My smiles
Timeless, but fleeting.

My tears
Endless, but bleeding.

My heart,
Quiet, but beating.

My worries
Few, but impeding.

My psyche,
Present, and seething.

My life
Temporary, but draining.

My body
Dying, but breathing.

28. Crybaby

It hurts so much,
I want to cry.
A cry baby having tears in her eyes.
Unpacking my heart with words,
The sobs pressing against my lungs,
Weighing down my heart.
My soul cries out,
Wanting something to alleviate
The pressure in my chest
That threatens to tear me apart.
Nevertheless, I cry these useless tears,
Keeping the pain of the past and
Present
Bottled up together inside.
Pitiful.
I'm just a crybaby,
Who only knows how to cry.

29. The Dark Bridal

On a lone mountain,
There lives a lone queen,
Her kingdom is quite lonelier than it
Seems.

Residing on her throne of thorns,
Her arms limp at rest,
Crimson tipped dripping forlorn,
Her body, a bloody mess.

Feelings flowing in waves of tidal,
Earning the title *The Dark Bridal.*

As the moon sets above the night sky,
She repeatedly asks herself this question,
"Why am I like this, why?"

As she caresses her long black dress,
She climbs of off her high seat.
She walks through the silent corridors
Wondering what fate she will meet.

Gracefully she glides.
Slowly is her stride.

Her arms raised high,
Her smile bitterly wide,
She embraces her groom
Who sits on his chair,
His head leaning down
His body lifeless instead.

She knows he's not there,
For he is off yonder.
She then walks away
To the palace, she wanders.

Her shoes leave a red trail
To match those already there,
For her mind is naught.
Her thoughts are strained.
Little does she know it,
She's gone.

She peers off her balcony
Looking at the sky.

Then comes her question
"Why, oh, why?"

All has been taken,

For none she has received.
Her husband, her kingdom,
All had her deceived.

And yet,
She lives in her wonderland
Sighing, but happy.

She doesn't quite understand
That her life is in her fingers
Trickling away.
She looks on
Not even afraid.

The moon is full.
The stars are gone.
The creatures of the night
Make a lovely song.

To add to her suffering
Her long list of regrets,
She laughs mad laughter
Then the end of her life is met.

Beauty

1. Uncertainty

Those same eyes burn with something
Unsaid.
A pot of water boiling above blue
Flames
Snowflakes melting against the
Pavement on a summer day.
Rain-soaked asphalt on a winter's night
Rain replacing the snow in the sky
The final moments of asphyxiation after
A breath of fresh air.
It's these moments of familiarity and
Uncertainty that cause words to go
From solid to gas.
Thoughts to hypertension and cold to
Burning.

2. Morning, Night

In the wake of the sun, there remains the
shadows that dance in unison with passing
Cars.
As the rays travel across the uneven
Surface of the cement,
The barrenness of the field remains,
Disappearing with the sunlight.
The colors change when I look away,
And each shade feels similar to one
Another.
In an endless gradient of simple colors.
Blue, Red,
And Yellow
Then Purple, Orange,
And Black.
I feel as if I can see everything.
With only one layer of the sky to see,
Can I see the stars anymore?

3. Night Run

I have the ability to time travel.
As time slows down when I run,
   I get lost in the night sky.

The sounds of the night
Echo off these unfinished walls
Of the lines of houses side by side.

My music beats softly, a comfort in the
Noisy silence.
I run beside the shadows,
And the shadows run alongside me.

The night feels more desolate than it
Feels alive.

My shoes against the concrete
The gravel, the grass,
The distance, the fatigue,
My lungs as I breathe,
The lights drift away.

REGRET

1. Neglect

Tell me the difference between reality and fantasy.
Maybe it is the unconscious desire to make one the
Other.
A little bit of reality remains in the
Little things left unforgotten.

Like...
Bitterness.

A crying child,
And her sleeping parent.

Then,
The empty crib.
The empty bed and
The empty house...
Listen.

The cries still echo through the halls,
And no one can sleep through the night.
It's almost blasphemous to say
No one cared.
A child isn't made of paper, porcelain, or plastic.
It is able to remember
To be broken, to be cracked, and to be ripped apart.
And it doesn't feel real
To be alive.

2. Repention

Wanting a hug is different
From giving a hug.
A brief moment of formality
Against extended periods of longing.

In silence,
I learned to cry
Without a sound.
Tears run down my cheeks.
I breathe in and out,
And try to settle, contain, keep
The pain inside.

I lower my voice
And wait for this moment to pass.

Otherwise, I don't feel as if I can *feel.*
As if the sadness could seep deeper still.
Where is the beat of my heart?
Monotone-colored silence threatens to
Tear my skin apart.

Again and again.
Let's make the same mistake again and
Again.

My tears are dried up,
And this regret is knotted inside me.

The beat I feel is fading-
Stop and stay for a while.
You remind me of when I truly was alive.
When my feelings were once wild.

The pure joy at the idea of youth,
And my own dementing truths.

Ignoring the child
Whom I gave this strife,
Carrying this baggage like a burden
On our backs, these few years of our lives.
Pray tell the reason why.

As I sit here alone, I sigh

At me
Who I was, and
Where I was before all this began.
When I remembered love,
And the soothing touch of a simple life, bland.

Like the essence of time in sand,
I don't think that I can
Continue on
Looking myself in the eyes.

Let my actions repent
And my heart redeem
Whatever I took away

From me.

3. Box of Music

I had a music box.
It was my music box.
A heart shaped box with a hollow inside
With a tiny ballerina that
Twirled in endless circles.

My thoughts and mind became the music.
One single, repeated tune
It was the only tune it was able to play.
Yet, I stood mesmerized by how the tune
Never became tired,
Nor did the little ballerina.
I could watch her dance as I listened to the
Melody, the chorus and the silence that
Centered around my
Heart...
Shaped...
Box.

All the while, I would watch the tiny
Ballerina dance.

I would watch her painted face
A simple, immeasurable beauty laid atop a
Spindle.
I would wind the key
Then watch and
Breathe.
Listen and forget.

I can remember feeling sad.
I can remember feeling lonely.
I can remember tracing the design with my hand.
My precious, little thing.
One day, a broken music box
By another's idle and little hands.
The box was as blue as the feeling in my heart.
My ballerina would never dance again.
Her painted face became blotchy.
A plastic, amalgamated figure laying on its side
With broken legs, still managing a smile at the loss.
I can remember the bitterness that settled inside,
That plucked a chord in my heart.
Yet my words can't replay that song in my memory.

4. As If...

Trying hard to forget
My feelings muddled inside
Murky, like a swamp bogged down by self-doubt,
Suffocated beneath the soft likeness of clay.

I thought it was love.
Arriving in the shallow depths of my heart,
Seeking to tend to.
Seeking to mend anew desire.

Laughter, never more suddenly kept than crept
In the birth of a dream.

A kind man, a wise man,
A tender, honest, driven man
From knowledge ran
Towards.

A tear, never there,
Never feared
That ache deep within my heart.

The longer it stays, the more it goes.

It grows. It starves. It dies.

To love, good-bye.

Fly free, spirit aglow.
To return to hide
To dream, to thrive.

If only...
Love's direction wasn't turned aside.

Senseless words, blinded by the mind.
And that tentative smile collapses to a frown
Nervous to believe in how much affection
You lack, then show
Cold expectation like any other ideal.
Words frozen over.
Is it real?

Emotionless.

I can't see you...

I can't feel you...

Like a memory drifting away.

5. Hopeless

Broken bones can be mended.
Personalities can switch.
However, I don't think that
One could ever be fixed.

Toys can be forgotten,
Broken and deceived.
However, no one can take away
All their plastic memories.

Trying to pick up all these pieces of mine
To put them back in my broken mind

Hour by hour
The clock never ceases to tick
Along with the beat of my heart
Slowly making me feel sick.

My brain is pounding against my head,
Telling me to stop thinking
About all these things that remain
In my heart that's still sinking.

No matter how much I plea,
My brain is a vortex.
Whether its taunting me during the day,
My brain is never at rest.

A little reminder of everything I did wrong
Playing at the back of my head
Like a sad lullaby's song.

Overcoming

1. You Deserve Better

Is it nice to know that
All your friends are talking about you,
And to have all your regrets wrapped around you,
And to wonder how you've ended up like this?

They're all I have even if they are like this.

Are they all you deserve?

But remember all
The hints given back then.

It's hard to keep a trusting heart
Inside a complex,
Worrying left and right.

Ask for an answer
And like all people,
Ask yourself questions to which
You already know the answers.

The lie is to be expected.
The truth is to be sought.

You decide.

2. Mirror, Mirror

What I see in the mirror
Reflects what the mirror sees.
But what if what the mirror reflects
Isn't the true me?

The beauty it doesn't see
That it shows to me
Doesn't show
How beautiful I can be.

The me
What I could be
Not reflected
By what the mirror sees.

If it was ugliness
That the mirror sees,
What if it doesn't see,
And It doesn't see my real beauty?

If it was weakness
That the mirror says is me
Then what if it doesn't show
That I am truly mighty?

● ● ●

Unfair
Isn't thee?
Showing lies
Three by three

All these faults
That I don't see
What the mirror says
Is truly me.

To be or not to be,
Of what I see is key
Because what I am to be
Not what the mirror sees

To be who I can be.

What I see in the mirror
Is what the mirror sees,
But I know what the mirror reflects,
Isn't the true me.

3. *Believe*

The world is made of broken
Memories.
We have all lost something we
Love
Surrender to an all sovereign
Power
And believe in what is above.

When there's nothing else to do,
For the comfort of your soul,
Let down the burden you carry,
Rather than let your heart turn
Cold.

4. Human

I think it's blasphemy.
How I told myself how I had to
Be.
Perfection made without a flaw,
Not a painting, but a masterpiece.

Humans are more like unfinished
Works of art.
A half-drawn doodle on lined
Paper
A misaligned dot on a canvas
That was able to become
Something more.

ABOUT THE AUTHOR

I.D. Rose (Samantha Derisse) is a young woman who resides in a suburban city in Indiana. She discovered her passion for poetry at a very young age, and her book *Mental Prison* is the compilation of poems that she began writing in her childhood all the way into her young adult years. Her desire is that her poetry will inspire others to write down what they feel as a way of self-expression to help them overcome any obstacles they may face.

For book signings and speaking engagements,

contact I.D. Rose at

rosewaterfairy@gmail.com

or

shamegha074@gmail.com

Follow I.D Rose on Instagram:
an_idle_rosepetal

MORE POETRY
COMING SOON:

When the Conscience Speaks

All books by I.D. Rose are available in print & digitally on kindle.com

You can also find them at Amazon.com, Barnes&Noble.com, and everywhere great poetry is sold.

www.ingramcontent.com/pod-product-compliance
Lightning Source LLC
Chambersburg PA
CBHW060350090426
42734CB00011B/2099